COMMON CORE CLINICS

Grade 4

English Language Arts

CLINICS

Reading Informational Text

Common Core Clinics, English Language Arts, Reading Informational Text, Grade 4
OT231 / 343NA

ISBN-13: 978-0-7836-8478-9

Cover Image: © Image Source/Photolibrary

Triumph Learning® 136 Madison Avenue, 7th Floor, New York, NY 10016

© 2012 Triumph Learning, LLC
Coach is an imprint of Triumph Learning®

ALL ABOUT YOUR BOOK

COMMON CORE CLINICS will help you master important reading skills.

Each lesson has a **Learn About It** box that teaches the idea. A sample passage focuses on the skill. A **graphic organizer** shows you a reading strategy.

Each lesson has a **Try It** passage with **guided reading**.

 **Higher-Order Thinking Skills**

Questions that make you think further about what you read.

Apply It provides **independent practice** for reading passages, answering short-answer questions, and responding to writing prompts.

Table of Contents

Main Idea and Supporting Details

Learn About It

The **main idea** of a passage is what it is mostly about. The author's main idea is his or her message to the reader about the topic of the passage. **Details** in the passage, such as examples or comparisons, explain and support the main idea. Often a writer will state the main idea, but it also might be implied, or hinted at, throughout the passage.

Read the passage. Look for a main idea statement. Then look for details that support it.

Icebergs form in all different shapes and sizes. Many have rounded tops like mountains, but others can be in the shape of a solid square block. Some icebergs are small, but most of them are huge. Icebergs in the North Atlantic Ocean average about 800 feet in height. The main source of icebergs is the glaciers of Greenland.

Main Idea			
Icebergs form in different shapes and sizes.			

Supporting Detail	Supporting Detail	Supporting Detail	Supporting Detail
Rounded tops	Shape of a solid, square block	Some small; most huge	Average about 800 feet in height

Detail That Does Not Support Main Idea
The main source of icebergs is the glaciers of Greenland.

Try It

Read the passage. Underline the details that tell you about the main idea. Remember, the main idea is not always stated. Use the questions to help you.

The Fox

A fox is an animal that looks like a medium-size dog. It has thin legs, a long nose, and pointed ears. The most common fox is the red fox. It is covered with a reddish coat and has a bushy tail. The smallest fox is the fennec fox. It weighs about 3.5 pounds.

Because the fox is a nighttime creature, you are not likely to see it during the day. You will have to wait until dark. During the day, the fox sleeps in an underground home called a *den*. At night, it hunts alone for its food. The fox uses its keen sense of hearing to look for mice, rabbits, insects, birds, and other small animals. Sometimes, foxes can help control pests on a farm.

> What is the main idea of the second paragraph? Which details in the paragraph support the main idea?

You are more likely to hear a fox during the nighttime as well. You will know one is nearby because of its high-pitched bark or eerie wail. Foxes also make other sounds, like warning calls. Additionally, a young fox asks for attention from its mother with a small bark.

> Sometimes the main idea is not stated. What is the main idea of the final paragraph?

A newborn fox is called a *cub*. Fox cubs are small with black fur all over their bodies. For the first few weeks of life, the cubs' mothers rarely leave their sides. At four weeks, the cubs begin to venture outside, but they stay very close to the den. These small creatures are extremely active at this young age. They play with and chase one another. By twelve weeks, they begin to learn to look for food by themselves, and by ten months, they are fully grown.

HOTS Evaluate

How do supporting facts back up the main idea of this passage?

Apply It

Read the passage. Look for main ideas and details. Answer the questions on the next page.

Water Striders

Imagine yourself zooming across the top of a pond or lake without sinking in. While this might be hard for *you* to do, it is easy for a water strider!

A water strider is a water bug that looks like a large mosquito. What makes it different from a mosquito, however, is the fact that it can walk across the water. You can find water striders on the surface of some ponds, marshes, and still water.

Water striders do more than just walk across the water. They also catch and eat their meals on the water, as well. Additionally, because they spend more of their time on the water, water striders feed mostly on other insects that live near water. In fact, water striders only go inland when rain or strong winds force them off the water.

The design of a water strider's body makes it easy for the insect to walk on the water. Its body is only one-half inch long, and it is covered with scales that keep it from getting heavy and sinking. Like all insects, the water strider has six legs. The front pair of legs is short while the middle and back legs are very long. These longer legs can spread over a larger area of water and are useful for rowing and steering across the water. No one leg is heavy enough to sink the insect.

Water striders also have very good vision and can move quickly. These traits help keep them from becoming prey, or food, for other insects.

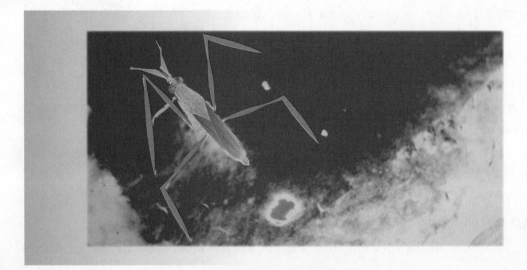

Answer these questions about "Water Striders." Write your answers in complete sentences.

1. How does the author use comparisons to support the main idea of the second paragraph?

   _____

   _____

2. The fourth paragraph is mainly about how a water strider's legs help it walk on the water. Name one detail that supports this.

   _____

   _____

3. The fifth paragraph talks about certain qualities water striders have that help them avoid their predators. Name one detail that supports this.

   _____

   _____

4. What is one detail from the passage that supports the main idea that a water strider is designed for walking on water?

   _____

   _____

5. Write a main idea statement for the passage.

   _____

LESSON 2

Summarize Text

Learn About It

> When you **summarize** text, you describe the main ideas and the important details of a passage in your own words. Answering *who, what, when, where, why,* and *how* questions can help you summarize. Summarizing is a good way to remember information.

Read the passage. Use the main idea and the important details to summarize.

Manatees are gentle, slow-moving sea creatures. They live in the warm waters of coastal areas. They only eat plants. Since they are mammals, they cannot breathe underwater and, instead, must come to the surface for air. Life can be dangerous for manatees. Many of them are injured by boats. Others get caught in fishing lines. Manatees are sometimes known as "sea cows."

Summary Statement

Manatees are water mammals that eat plants. They live in warm waters. Many of them are injured by boats or fish lines.

Supporting Detail	**Supporting Detail**	**Supporting Detail**	**Supporting Detail**
Live in warm water	Eat plants	Mammals	Many injured by boats or fishing lines

Detail That Does Not Belong in Summary
Sometimes known as "sea cows"

Try It

Read the passage. Underline the main ideas and details that you would use to summarize the information. Use the questions to help you.

Mount Rushmore

Mount Rushmore National Memorial, located near Keystone, South Dakota, is an awe-inspiring monument. Each year, millions of people visit the site in order to gaze upon the incredible structure. Most visitors wonder, "What am I looking at? And *how* was it created?"

Mount Rushmore National Memorial is made up of the faces of four United States presidents carved into the side of a mountain. The presidents whose faces are sculpted in stone are George Washington, Thomas Jefferson, Abraham Lincoln, and Theodore Roosevelt. These four men were chosen for a reason. Each of these presidents played an important role in American history. Two of them helped create our nation, one saved it during a time of crisis, and one was part of its great growth and progress.

> Reread this passage. Ask yourself *who*, *what*, and *where* questions. Use the answers to these questions to summarize the passage.

The carvings of each face are about 60 feet tall. Because they are so big, it took more than fourteen years to complete them. Each president's head is as tall as a six-story building.

> Which details would not be included in a summary of the passage?

More than 400 workers helped to create the carvings. The work was dangerous and conditions were hard. Workers often faced blazing heat and bitter cold, as strong winds beat against the side of the mountain.

Can you imagine having to climb 700 steps to get to work each day? That is what the Mount Rushmore workers had to do. The stairs were built so that they could reach the top of the mountain. Then, they were lowered by cable to work on the side of the mountain.

These workers must have known they were working on something that would last forever.

What are some other reasons the workers might have been willing to do such hard and dangerous work?

Apply It

Read the passage. Pay attention to the main ideas and details that will help you summarize the passage. Answer the questions on the next page.

Pandas in the Bamboo Forests

If you want to see a panda in its natural habitat, you will have to travel to the forests of China. This is where most pandas make their homes. In these forests, pandas can find bamboo. Bamboo is a tall grass that pandas need in order to survive.

Pandas eat between 30 and 60 pounds of bamboo every day. In fact, most of their days are spent looking for and eating this tall grass.

While most animals eat many different types of food and can adapt, or change, what they eat when they have to, this is not true for pandas. Bamboo makes up almost all of their diet.

The panda's habitat, or the place where it lives, is shrinking. It is being cleared away by developers so that new homes and farms can be built on the land. When the land is cleared, the bamboo supply is destroyed.

In addition to the rapid destruction of these bamboo forests, there is another problem with this plant. Sometimes bamboo plants just dry out and die. This is called a *die-off*. When this happens, there is not enough bamboo left for the pandas to eat. In 1970, a die-off left very little food for the pandas. More than 100 pandas died because of this. There was another die-off in 1983. This time, people stepped in to help. They found the starving pandas and helped feed them.

More and more, the people of China are learning how to protect pandas. They are taking steps to save the bamboo forests. If these bamboo forests are safe, then the pandas will be safe as well.

Answer these questions about "Pandas in the Bamboo Forests." Write your answers in complete sentences.

1. Write one detail about pandas found in the first paragraph.

_____

_____

2. Which detail in the second paragraph helps you summarize the information there?

_____

_____

3. What is a detail in the third paragraph that does not need to be included in a summary of that paragraph?

_____

_____

4. Which details in the passage tell you what happens when land is cleared for farms?

_____

_____

5. How can you best summarize the entire passage?

_____

_____

Historical Text

> **Historical text** tells readers about important people, places, events, and dates from the past. Readers learn what happened and why it happened.

Read the passage. Look for people, places, events, and dates as you read.

Sally Ride woke up early on the morning of June 18, 1983. It was an important day at the Kennedy Space Center. The space shuttle *Challenger* would be launched into space that day. Ride and four other crew members would be onboard. A whole year of hard work and training had led up to this day. She would soon become the first woman in space.

Historical Text Feature	Example
People	Sally Ride
Places	Kennedy Space Center
Events	Launch of **Challenger**
Dates	June 18, 1983

Try It

Read the passage. Underline ideas, dates, people, and events that you find in the historical text. Use the questions to help you.

The Pony Express

In 1860, something new came to the West. It was a new way of delivering the mail, known as the Pony Express. Young men began to carry mail on horseback across the frontier. It was an exciting job, but it could be extremely dangerous, too.

> Historical text tells what happened and why. What event does the passage tell about? Why did it happen?

Pony Express riders galloped from the East to the West. It was a journey of about 1,900 miles. They carried mail on their saddles. Riders changed horses every 10 to 15 miles. New riders took over after every 75 miles.

The Pony Express route was dangerous. Some riders were killed or wounded by bandits. Others were injured or became ill. Riders were slowed down by blizzards and snowstorms. Floods were a danger on the journey, too. Despite all of this, only *one* sack of mail was ever lost by the Pony Express!

> Historical text often includes dates. What dates do you see in the passage?

The first Pony Express trip took 10 days. Later trips averaged between 8 and 10 days. Before the Pony Express, people waited months for their mail to come. It was hard for them to believe that the Pony Express could be so fast! The fastest time ever recorded was 7 days, 17 hours. That was in 1861, when the Pony Express delivered copies of a speech made by President Lincoln.

The Pony Express lasted only 18 months. It ended in 1861, when the first telegraph line to the West was completed. Two days later, the Pony Express made its last trip. Now, people could send messages across the nation in minutes. The Pony Express became part of history.

HOTS Analyze

Why did the telegraph bring an end to the Pony Express?

Apply It

Read the passage. Look for people, places, ideas, and events from the past. Answer the questions on the next page.

The Underground Railroad

Despite its name, the Underground Railroad was not a *real* railroad. It was actually a secret system for enslaved people in the South to escape to freedom in the North. As many as 75,000 people used it between the years 1830 and 1860.

The Underground Railroad was not operated by any one person. Instead, it was made up of many different people, working in their own towns or homes. They hid people in safe places, fed them, and delivered them to the next safe place. In this way, the Railroad managed to move people northward.

Escapees did most of their moving at night. They would travel between 10 and 20 miles to the next station. They rested in barns or other concealed places until it was safe. Then, they moved on.

If money was needed, it was donated by people or groups. Some of these people helped in other ways, too, like finding the escapees work once they reached their new homes.

Even though the Underground Railroad was not a real railroad, it still used railroad terms. The places where escapees rested were called "stations." The route was run by "stationmasters" and a "conductor" moved people from one station to the next.

The journey was a frightening one for the escapees. They were in constant danger because people would be paid for capturing them and bringing them back to their owners.

Many people became famous because of their involvement with the Underground Railroad. One of these people was Harriet Tubman. She made nineteen trips into the South and brought as many as 300 enslaved people to freedom.

Answer these questions about "The Underground Railroad." Write your answers in complete sentences.

1. Which event in history is the passage about?

   _____

   _____

2. When was the Underground Railroad in operation?

   _____

   _____

3. Name a detail from the third paragraph that tells you how the Underground Railroad operated.

   _____

   _____

4. What is one detail from the fifth paragraph that describes a term used in the Underground Railroad?

   _____

   _____

5. How is the passage an example of historical text?

   _____

   _____

Scientific Text

Learn About It

Scientists look at the world and ask questions. When we read **scientific text**, we look for explanations of *what* happens in the world and *why* it happens. Reading scientific text helps you know more about the world around you.

Read the passage. Look for a scientific explanation of how or why something happens.

A forest is a habitat, or a place where plants and animals live. The largest plants in the forest are the trees. The tree leaves create an umbrella-like canopy over the rest of the forest. Other plants live in this shade. Grass does not grow on the forest floor. Instead, there are mosses and other plants that grow best in the shade.

Scientific Text Feature	Example
Looks at the world	Forest habitat
Asks questions	Who lives there? What grows there?
Explains what happens	Trees make shade. Plants live in shade. No grass grows, but mosses grow.
Explains why it happens	Mosses and some plants grow best in shade.

Try It

Read the passage. Underline the scientific details that help you know more about the world around you. Use the questions to help you.

Temperate Grasslands

About thirty percent of the world is made up of a habitat known as the "temperate grasslands." Most of the temperate grasslands in the world are found in nine countries, including the United States. This grass-covered habitat is home to a wide variety of plant and animal life.

> What does the passage describe?

The temperate grassland is hot in the summer and cold in the winter. From a distance, all of the grasses may look the same. However, if you look closely, you will find several different kinds of plants in this habitat. A grassland habitat is made up of grasses, hundreds of wildflowers, and other plants and animals.

A grassland is a sunny place, but it can also be very windy. Grassland plants often need a lot of sun to survive and are not harmed by strong winds. You will rarely see trees in a grassland because there is simply not enough water there for them to thrive.

> The passage tells which plants and animals live in a grassland. Why do these animals live there?

In just a small area of a grassland, you can find many different types of living things. Insects, such as grasshoppers and beetles, make their homes here. You can also find birds, mice, and other small animals, such as prairie dogs. Prairie dogs look like squirrels, but without the bushy tails. They can be seen burrowing into the ground. Larger animals such as coyotes, wolves, foxes, and badgers also live in the grasslands.

All of these different plants and animals find food and shelter in a grassland habitat.

 **Analyze**

Why does the phrase "sea of grass" describe a grassland?

Apply It

Read the passage. Look for explanations of what happens. Answer the questions on the next page.

Twister!

A tornado is a tall column of rapidly spinning air that extends out from a thunderstorm and touches the ground. It looks like a long tube or a big, spiraling tunnel. It is wide at the top and narrow at the bottom. A tornado can last for a few minutes or sweep across the land for miles. For good reasons, tornadoes are often called "twisters."

Tornadoes start as severe thunderstorms, usually in late spring and summer. Hot, moist air begins to rise rapidly from the ground. Changing temperatures cause the rising air to whirl. This forms a long, funnel-shaped cloud that reaches the ground.

Tornadoes produce fast, strong winds that can cause tremendous amounts of damage. Sometimes, the winds are so strong that they can lift cars and buses into the air and blow the roofs off houses. Tornado winds can cause branches to break off trees and even uproot some trees completely! Even small objects can become dangerous during a twister, especially when they are blown through the air at such high speeds.

Scientists measure the strength of a tornado by using the Enhanced Fujita Scale (EF Scale). It ranks tornadoes from EF0 to EF5, based on wind speed. EF0 and EF1 are weaker tornadoes. EF2 and EF3 are stronger, but it is the EF4 and EF5 tornadoes that are *really* destructive.

There are more tornadoes in the United States than anywhere else in the world. While many of these are smaller tornadoes and do not cause a lot of damage, a major tornado can be a true danger.

Answer these questions about "Twister!" Write your answers in complete sentences.

1. What scientific event does the passage explain?

   _____

   _____

2. What do the details in the second paragraph tell about?

   _____

   _____

3. Which details in the passage tell about the damage tornadoes cause?

   _____

   _____

4. Find details that explain how tornadoes are measured.

   _____

   _____

5. How did the passage help you know more about the world around you?

   _____

   _____

Technical Text

Learn About It

Technical text is a type of informational text that explains the steps for how to do something. When you read technical text, pay attention to the information that tells you what you need and what steps to take.

Read the passage. Look for steps that tell you how to do something.

When you are riding a bike, it is important to signal a turn or stop so that other bike riders know what you are about to do. Always check behind you before you signal.

Left Turn: Hold your left arm straight out.
Stop: Bend your elbow and point your left arm downward, in an L shape.
Right Turn: Bend your elbow and point your left arm upward, in an L shape.

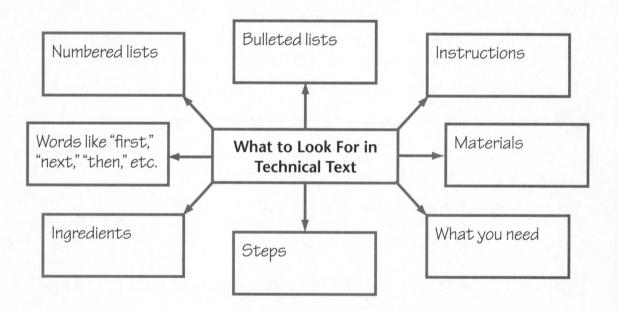

Numbered lists

Bulleted lists

Instructions

Words like "first," "next," "then," etc.

What to Look For in Technical Text

Materials

Ingredients

Steps

What you need

Try It

Read the passage. Look for the steps that tell you what to do. Use the questions to help you.

How to Paint a Bookcase

Materials:
- 1 bookcase
- 1 can of paint
- a tarp or newspaper
- old clothes that can get dirty
- a three-inch brush and a one-inch brush

Directions:
1. Dip the one-inch brush into the paint. Drag the brush on the inside edge of the can to remove extra paint and avoid drips. Repeat as needed.
2. Paint along all the creases of the shelves on the top, bottom, and sides.
3. Dip the wide brush into the paint and remove any extra paint. Repeat as needed.
4. Paint the back, top, and sides of the bookshelf in long, even swipes. Try to make all your brush strokes go in the same direction.
5. Once the creases are dry, use the wide brush to cover all unpainted areas.
6. Leave the bookshelf to dry in fresh air. The smell will be strong, so opening a window is very important.
7. Immediately seal the paint cans. Wipe up any spills and rinse your brushes in a sink.
8. After the bookcase is completely dry, carefully remove the tarp or newspaper. Remember, drying can take up to 24 hours.

> How do the directions tell you what you need in order to paint a bookcase?

> You need to know which order to complete these steps in to successfully paint a bookcase. What part of the text tells you the correct order to follow?

Why do the directions tell you to seal the paint cans immediately?

Apply It

Read the passage. Think about what you need to have and what you need to do. Answer the questions on the next page.

A Garden in a Bottle

If the idea of having your own indoor garden sounds like fun, you should try growing plants in a bottle! Plants that like to grow in damp, shady places are best for bottle gardens. Most small ferns and mosses usually grow in corners, under trees, or near walls, so they make great bottle garden plants. The bottle garden will provide what they need to live and grow—water, air, light, and warmth.

Materials:
- big glass jar with a wide neck
- small stones or gravel
- potting soil
- different kinds of mosses
- water
- spray bottle

Directions:
1. Put a thin layer of stones or gravel in the bottom of the jar.
2. Pour a thick layer of soil over the gravel. Press it down.
3. Place the moss on the top of the soil. Press it down, lightly.
4. Add water to your garden using the spray bottle.
5. Put your garden in a place where it will receive some light, but do not put it in direct sunlight, or else it will dry out.

When your garden gets dry, spray it with water from the spray bottle.

Enjoy your garden!

Answer these questions about "A Garden in a Bottle." Write your answers in complete sentences.

1. How does the passage tell what you need to gather together before you begin making your garden?

_____

_____

2. Which detail in the first paragraph tells you where to find mosses?

_____

_____

3. Which part of the passage tells you the steps you need to take in order to create the garden?

_____

_____

4. What do you do after you have finished putting your moss in the garden?

_____

_____

5. Which details in the passage tell you that your plants need water?

_____

_____

Drawing and Supporting Inferences

Learn About It

An **inference** is an educated guess a reader can make, based on the information he or she already has. It is not information that is directly stated in the passage. Details in a text give readers information. They may use this information, along with their own prior knowledge, to draw an inference.

Read the passage. Look for the information that helps you make an inference about it.

> Chimpanzees are a species of great apes that live in Africa. They live in groups of fifteen to twenty members, called communities. They enjoy being together. When they meet, they often greet each other with kisses, a hug, or a pat on the back. Sometimes, they even hold hands. When they are together, their contact is mostly peaceful and friendly.

Facts and Details	Facts and Details	Facts and Details	Facts and Details
Live in groups	Enjoy being together	Greet each other	Contact with each other is peaceful

Inference
Chimpanzees are very social animals.

Try It

Read the passage. Underline the details that help you make an inference about the topic. Use the questions to help you.

Learning a Trade

Life was not easy for people living during colonial times. Young people needed to learn skills so they could find work, make money, and help support their families. One way to do this was to become an apprentice, or a person who learns a skill by training with an expert. This was a good way to learn carpentry, shoemaking, and many other professions.

> The writer includes details about what an apprentice had to do. What do you think the writer is inferring about the life of an apprentice?

Because there was a high demand for things like furniture, shoes, tools, and wheels, people could make money by producing these things in the colonies. Young boys between the ages of ten and fifteen years old would spend time with people who specialized in each of these areas and learn the tricks of the trade. They became apprentices to these experts.

> The writer mentions that, eventually, many apprentices could open their own shops. What is the writer inferring about being an apprentice by doing this?

Apprentices served their "masters," or teachers, for four to seven years. They left their own homes and went to live with these masters. Even though they were not paid, they were given food, clean clothing, and a place to sleep. In exchange for this, they had to do whatever the master needed done. They worked long hours, but were willing to do this in order to learn a trade they could someday practice on their own.

At the end of their apprenticeship, apprentices often created a finished product. This was judged by the master. If the master approved of the product, apprentices began a new life. They traveled to nearby villages to make or repair things. People throughout the area learned about them and their work. After a certain amount of time, they could open their own shops and make a living.

HOTS Analyze

Why do you think that a young person would decide that becoming an apprentice was a worthwhile activity?

Apply It

Read the passage. Look for clues that help you make inferences. Answer the
questions on the next page.

Dogs Are Good for You

Dogs are often called "man's best friend." They are loyal, fun-loving animals.
Owning a dog can be a great experience. But, for many people, there are even
more important reasons to own a dog. Many experts believe that owning a dog
can be good for the general well-being of you and your family.

We all know that some dogs make great watch dogs for families. They are
good at warning us about potential danger by barking. But, they also bring
something else to a family. A family works together caring for a dog. Family
members share tasks like feeding and walking the dog. They also share the loyalty
and joy that a dog gives back to them.

In order to enjoy having a dog as a pet, you
need to keep your dog healthy. But, did you
know that caring for your dog can keep you
healthy, too? Most dog owners spend a lot of
time caring for their dogs. They take them
for long walks and enjoy playtime together
in the park. These things can provide a great
health benefit for both the dog and the
dog's owner. In fact, when you first get
a dog, you may find yourself exercising
more than you ever have before.

While a dog may be your "best
friend," owning a dog is also a way
to make new friends. Walking your
dog, taking it to training classes, and
playing at dog runs are all great ways to meet
other people who share your interests and love of dogs.

Answer these questions about "Dogs Are Good for You." Write your answers in complete sentences.

1. What is the topic of the passage? How does the title help you know what the passage is about?

_____

_____

2. The writer infers that owning a pet helps a family work together. Which details show this?

_____

_____

3. How does keeping a dog healthy keep you healthy?

_____

_____

4. How can owning a dog help you meet new people?

_____

_____

5. What can you infer about the writer after reading this passage?

_____

_____

Academic Vocabulary

Learn About It

When we read science, social studies, or math texts, we encounter special words that are specific to that subject matter. We need to know the meaning of these words to fully understand the passage. Clues can help you. When you read **academic text**, look for definitions, examples, synonyms, antonyms, and other context clues to help you understand the meaning of unfamiliar words.

Read the passage. Look for ways to help you figure out unknown words.

A **map** is a drawing on a flat surface. It shows a region, or area. Floor plans, directions, and road routes can all be shown on maps. Maps take the real, round world and display it on a flat surface. Areas can be distorted. Their size, shape, and locations may not be accurate. Trying to correctly represent Earth's curved surface on a flat, piece of paper is not easy.

Clue Type	Example(s)
Definition	A drawing on a flat surface
Examples	Floor plans, directions, road routes
Context	Distorted—Their size, shape, and locations may not be accurate.

Try It

Read the passage. Look for clues to help you understand academic words. Use the questions to help you.

Surviving the Sahara!

The sun beats down. There are no clouds in the sky. The **temperature** is extremely high. This is the Sahara Desert, one of the driest and hottest places on Earth. You might be wondering how anything can survive here. There are many different ways that people and animals beat the heat.

> Academic words are often in boldface. Which word in the first paragraph is in boldface? Use other clues in the paragraph to tell its meaning.

The fennec fox lives in the Sahara Desert. In many parts of the Sahara, there is nothing but sand for miles. In order to escape the hot sunlight, the fennec fox digs a long **burrow**, or hole, under the sand. It sleeps there during the heat of the day. At night, when it is cool enough to hunt for food, it leaves the burrow.

Silver ants also live in the desert. They escape the heat of the Sahara by clinging onto plants a few inches above the sand, where temperatures are cool enough to survive.

Certain people also find ways to survive in the Sahara. They have **adapted** their behaviors. Their activities, clothing, and shelter are all chosen to cope with the extreme heat. During the middle of the day, they stay sheltered. When they go out, they wear loose clothing to keep themselves cool. Their houses are designed to keep cool air inside.

Several rivers flow beneath the Sahara. At an **oasis**, or a green area, a spring brings this water to the surface. People survive by learning where water is and staying close to it. Travelers go from one oasis to another. The Sahara is so big that travelers may go days before reaching an oasis. Knowing this helps them plan their route.

> What helps you understand the meaning of the word *oasis* in the fifth paragraph?

What other things might people do to stay cool in the desert?

Apply It

Read the passage. Be on the look out for academic words and clues that will help you understand what they mean. Answer the questions on the next page.

What Do Scientists Do?

Imagine that you are walking through a park one day and you see a nest in a tree. You wonder about it—How did it get there? What is it made of? What kind of animal does it belong to?

Do you want to know more about the things around you? Do you try to learn about them? If so, you are acting like a **scientist**. Scientists ask questions and look for answers about the world around them.

In order to learn more about something, scientists **observe** it. When you observe something, you

study it carefully. You watch closely to see if anything changes and take notes. Remember the nest in the tree? As you watch it, you might see something change. For example, you might see what bird comes along to use it.

Scientists use special **tools** for observation. Field glasses, hand lenses, and microscopes are all tools that make things look bigger. Scientists also measure the things they observe. Tools like thermometers, rulers, and stopwatches are used to measure different things.

How do scientists learn more about their findings? One way is to compare them. When you **compare** things, you see if they are similar or different. For example, when you observe the nest, you can compare it to other nests, to see if it is similar in size or shape. Sometimes it takes hours, days, or even years for scientists to answer the questions they are asking! They need to remember what they have done so that they can analyze their results. They **record**, or write down, their observations in a lab notebook.

Answer these questions about "What Do Scientists Do?" Write your answers in complete sentences.

1. What is the topic of the passage? How does the title help you know this?

_____

_____

2. Which academic word is in the third paragraph? What does it mean? What told you the meaning?

_____

_____

3. Tools are things that are used to do something. How do you know this?

_____

_____

4. What are some tools that scientists use to measure things?

_____

_____

5. How does the use of academic words in the passage help you better understand the topic being discussed?

_____

_____

Chronology

Learn About It

Chronology is the order of events in which things occur. It helps us know what happens and when it happens. Dates and times tell you about chronology. Numbered lists, directions, and instructions are often written in chronological order. Words like *next, then, now, soon, after, yesterday,* and *later* all provide us with chronological information.

Read the passage. Look for words that help you know chronology.

Your body makes a shadow. It blocks the light. When the light changes, your shadow changes. Let's see how the sunlight changes a shadow.

First, go outside in the morning sun. Next, ask a friend to trace your shadow. Then, measure it. How many centimeters long is your shadow? Do this again at noon. How did your shadow change? What do you think made it change?

Chronology	Example
Words that explain sequence or order of events	First, next, then
Words that tell a date or time	Morning, noon

Try It

Read the passage. Look for lists and words that help you know the chronology. Use the questions to help you.

Flight Begins!

In June 1783, the first hot air balloon lifted into the air. As a crowd watched, it flew over a mile. A few months later, another balloon took off. This one was carrying animals. Later, another one was able to carry people!

> **What are some important dates and times mentioned in this passage?**

Balloons were fun, but more work was needed before people could truly fly. Then, in 1804, came the glider. The glider was a device that had wings like today's airplane, but no engine. Gliders used the wind to float in the air. Two brothers in the United States read about this glider and got some ideas about flying machines. They were the Wright brothers.

Wilbur and Orville Wright wanted to build a flying machine of their own. They read all they could about the flying machines that already existed, and then they made a plan. They hoped to build a glider that people could steer. After lots of hard work, they were successful.

They worked on their glider in Kitty Hawk, North Carolina, for three years. Even then, it was still difficult to steer. Then, the brothers solved this by building an engine for the glider.

> **Which words in the passage tell you about chronology?**

On December 14, 1903, they flipped a coin to decide who would get to fly their new glider first. Wilbur won. The glider flew for only a few seconds. A few days later, it flew again! This time it flew 120 feet in the air.

The Wright brothers did not stop working on their project. In 1908, they built a machine that flew for an hour. Because of them, people could now fly!

 **Understand**

How does the Wright brothers' flying machine compare to a modern-day airplane?

Apply It

Read the passage. Be on the look out for words that tell chronology. Answer the questions on the next page.

Stars and Stripes

You probably see the American flag flying on schools and other buildings every day. On the Fourth of July, it is displayed proudly throughout the country. There is even an American flag on the moon! The flag you are looking at today has thirteen stripes and fifty stars. However, it did not always look like this.

In the 1600s, America was just a group of colonies under the rule of another country, Great Britain. In 1776, the colonists fought a war to become an independent nation. To represent their new, self-governing country, they decided that they needed a flag. They chose one with thirteen stripes and thirteen stars, one of each for every colony that existed at the time.

After the war was won, the new, independent country began to grow. Soon, two more states joined the nation. By 1818, there were twenty states. Leaders thought that adding a star and a stripe to the flag each time a state was added would not work. They decided instead that the flag would always have thirteen stripes. Only a new star would be added with each new state.

By 1912, the United States was made up of forty-eight states. In that year, the president ordered that all the stars on the flag should look the same. The last big change to the American flag was in 1959, when two states, Alaska and Hawaii, were added to the country. In turn, two stars were added to the flag. This flag, with fifty stars, is the flag we fly today.

Answer these questions about "Stars and Stripes." Write your answers in complete sentences.

1. What is the topic of the passage?

_____

_____

2. How many stars and stripes did the first American flag have?

_____

_____

3. In the second paragraph, which words help explain the chronology of the events?

_____

_____

4. As the country changed, so did the flag. What information in the third paragraph tells you this?

_____

_____

5. How does understanding chronology help readers know more about the American flag?

_____

_____

Comparison and Contrast

Learn About It

One way to better understand what you read is to **compare** details and information. When you compare, you think about how things are the *same*. When you **contrast**, you think about how things are *different*.

Read the passage. Look for information that shows how things are alike and different.

The sun and the moon are two objects in our solar system that appear similar when we see them in the sky, but they are actually quite different. The sun is approximately 400 times the size of the moon and is much, much hotter! While the moon revolves around Earth, the sun is the central point of our solar system, so all other planets revolve around it.

Sun
400 times the size of the moon

Much hotter than the moon

Does not revolve around anything

Both
Are objects in our solar system

Look similar to us when we see them in the sky

Moon
Smaller than the sun

Colder than the sun

Revolves around Earth

Try It

Read the passage. Underline the details that help you make comparisons. Use the questions to help you.

Flightless Birds

Four of the world's largest species of birds are flightless. This means that they cannot fly. They do not have the same muscles in their chests that give other birds the power to soar through the air.

The most well-known of these flightless birds is the ostrich. Another flightless bird, the emu, is not as familiar to people, but it is just as unusual.

> These two birds are unusual. What is one thing about them that makes them different from most birds?

Ostriches are great big birds! They are the largest living birds. An average ostrich may weigh more than 345 pounds and be about 9 feet tall. The ostrich is an odd-looking bird, too. It has large eyes, a pink beak, brown feathers, and long white legs. It differs from all other birds by having two toes on each foot.

The emu is not as large as an ostrich, but it is still very big! The average emu weighs about 80 pounds and stands about 4 feet tall. It has dull brown feathers, a brown bill, and extremely long legs.

> Both of these birds are very fast runners. Find the details that tell you this.

An ostrich cannot fly, but it can run very fast! On the flat land of the African plains, an ostrich is able to run up to 40 miles per hour. Speed and extra-sharp eyesight help them escape from predators such as lions and hunters. Once cornered, an ostrich cannot fly away to save itself, but it can kick.

An emu is fast, too, but not as fast as an ostrich. It can run about 30 miles per hour where it lives on the grassy plains of Australia. Emus cause trouble for Australian farmers and ranchers. They destroy crops and even knock down fences.

 **Understand**

How does the habitat of the two birds differ?

Apply It

Read the passage. Look for details that tell how these two places are the same and different. Answer the questions on the next page.

New York City Landmarks

New York City is a great place to visit. There is so much to see! However, out of all the tourist hotspots, there are two sights that should *not* be missed. They are the Statue of Liberty and the Empire State Building. These places are symbolic for both the city and the country. Every year, millions of people visit these two historic landmarks.

The Statue of Liberty is on Liberty Island in the New York Harbor. The statue is of a woman holding a torch in her right hand and a tablet, or book, in her left hand. There are twenty-five windows in the crown of the statue. At night, they reflect light and shine like jewels across the water.

Lady Liberty, as the statue is sometimes called, is 151 feet tall and weighs 225 tons. It stands on a base that is 154 feet high. An elevator in the pedestal carries visitors to the base of the statue.

When the Empire State Building opened in 1933, it made history. It was the tallest building in the world at that time. It took 18 months, $24 million dollars, and more than 3,000 workers to build! It is 1,250 feet tall, which is almost quarter of a mile high! It has 103 floors. There are 6,500 windows in the building. It even has its own zip code!

Visitors can ride an elevator to the 86th floor and look out at the entire city and beyond. At night, the top of the building is lit with different colors. On the Fourth of July, it shines red, white, and blue.

Answer these questions about "New York City Landmarks." Write your answers in complete sentences.

1. Which two places does the passage compare and contrast?

_____

_____

2. Which details in first paragraph make a comparison between the Empire State Building and the Statue of Liberty?

_____

_____

3. Which details compare the height of the two places?

_____

_____

4. Name two details from the passage that explain how the two places are different.

_____

_____

5. How did comparing and contrasting the Empire State Building and the Statue of Liberty help you learn more about each historical landmark?

_____

_____

Cause and Effect

Learn About It

> When you look for **cause and effect** in a passage, you try to find how one thing leads to another. A *cause* is why something in the text happens. An *effect* is the result of that happening. Words like *so*, *because*, and *since* help you identify cause and effect.

Read the passage. Think about cause and effect—what happens and why it happens.

Earth's largest living land animal is the African elephant. Sadly, these creatures are in danger of becoming extinct. They are hunted for their ivory tusks. They are killed by farmers in order to stop them from eating their crops. Additionally, they have lost much of their habitat, or the place where they live. It is being cleared for farmland.

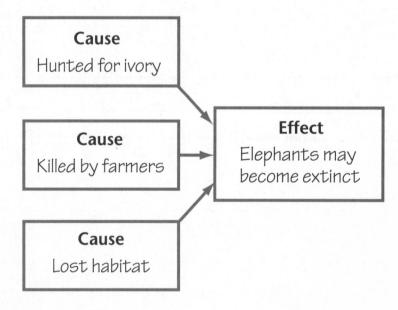

Cause
Hunted for ivory

Cause
Killed by farmers

Cause
Lost habitat

Effect
Elephants may become extinct

Try It

Read the passage. Underline the details that illustrate cause and effect.
Use the questions to help you.

The Amazing Beetle

Beetles are amazing creatures. Although they may seem rather ordinary, beetles are actually very special. The beetle has been around on this planet for millions of years. This is much longer than many other organisms. Why have they survived this long? It is because they have adapted, or changed, in ways that help them survive in shifting environments.

> What caused beetles to have been around for millions of years?

Many beetles have bodies that are adapted to where they live. For example, desert beetles have long legs that help keep them high above the hot desert sand. Likewise, beetles that live on the water have curved legs which they use as paddles to help them move in the water.

The whirligig beetle lives on the surface of ponds and streams. While it must look for food to survive, it must also be aware of its many predators. Because of this, the whirligig beetle has special eyes that are in two parts. The top part of the eye sees objects *on* the water, while the bottom part of the eye finds food *below* the water.

> What is the effect of beetle eggs hatching in cotton plants?

Other types of beetles live on cotton plants. They are perfectly suited for this home. They have long, thin noses that they use to drill holes into the leaves of the plants. They lay their eggs in these holes. When the eggs hatch into larvae, the larvae grow into adult insects and feed on the cotton plant.

Because of their incredibly adaptive nature, it is no wonder that many scientists believe that beetles are one of the most successful animals that have ever lived.

HOTS Analyze

How does thinking about cause and effect help you understand the topic?

Apply It

Read the passage. Look for causes and effects as you read. Answer the questions on the next page.

The California Gold Rush

Gold is a very rare precious metal that is only found in a few parts of the world. The discovery of gold usually sets off a "gold rush." This is when people flock to an area to join the search.

One of the biggest gold rushes of all time happened in California in 1848. Gold was discovered near San Francisco. News swept across the country and by 1849, the rush was on! Hundreds of thousands of eager miners began moving west. Grocers, doctors, blacksmiths, and farmers all headed for California. Because the year was 1849, these people became known as "forty-niners."

In the gold fields, the miners lived in tents and shacks. Each would stake a claim on an area of ground and start digging. It was hard work, usually with little success. Outlaws flocked to the camps. They stole gold and harmed miners. Since there were no police, there was nothing to stop them.

Some "forty-niners" grew rich without doing any digging. Gold hunters needed food and supplies, so businesspeople opened stores in these areas. They sold tents, clothes, and all the tools needed for mining gold. Prices for many things soared, since miners had no choice but to buy them.

Because of this sudden increase in population, the city of San Francisco grew and prospered. Tents and cabins were replaced by stores and hotels, and people settled down to make permanent homes there.

Most of the "forty-niners" never found the riches they dreamed of, but because of them, life in the West was forever changed.

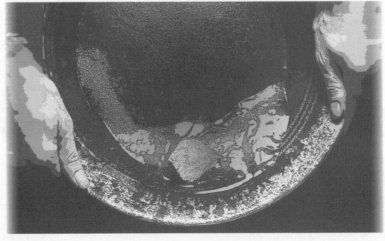

Answer these questions about "The California Gold Rush." Write your answers in complete sentences.

1. What event is described in the passage?

   _____

   _____

2. What was the cause of so many people moving west in 1849?

   _____

   _____

3. Which details from the passage tell you that life was hard for the miners? What caused it to be so hard?

   _____

   _____

4. How did the sudden increase in the number of people living in the West affect the city of San Francisco?

   _____

   _____

5. How do the causes and effects help you understand the California Gold Rush?

   _____

   _____

LESSON 11

Problem and Solution

Learn About It

One way to get information from a text is to look at **problems and solutions**. Think about what problems occur and how they occur. Then look at how they are solved.

Read the passage. Find the problem and the solution.

A desert is a hot, dry climate, which makes it difficult for animals to survive. Camels can survive in a desert, though. Their long legs keep their bodies away from the heat of the sand. Their wide feet keep them from sinking into the sand. Most camels can survive in the desert for a long time without water. Some can go a week without water, but others can survive for as long as a month!

Problem	Solutions
It is difficult for an animal to survive in the desert.	Long legs keep heat from a camel's body. Wide feet keep camels from sinking. Camels can go without water for long periods of time.

Try It

Read the passage. Underline the details that help you understand the problems and solutions. Use the questions to help you.

Building the Golden Gate Bridge

The city of San Francisco is separated from a nearby county by a deep channel, or body of water. This channel is known as the Golden Gate. At one time, the only way to cross this channel was by boat. The trip was slow, and the rough waters and strong winds made the voyage dangerous. People wanted to build a bridge over this channel, but they thought it was impossible.

> The location of the bridge caused problems. What were some of these problems?

An engineer named Joseph Strauss did not agree. He had designed more than 400 bridges in his lifetime. While none of them were as big as this one would be, he was determined to build the Golden Gate Bridge.

Work began on January 5, 1933. Thousands of people worked on the bridge. Divers dug under the deep, dangerous water. Others worked high up on the cables that connected the bridge's towers.

Strauss knew that the work was very dangerous, so he made sure the workers were provided with helmets. Safety nets were also strung below them, in case they fell.

> What was one problem that Strauss was concerned about? What did he do about it?

Another problem was that the 1930s were the days of the Great Depression. Though money was scarce, the city of San Francisco found a way to make it happen. As a result, the bridge project provided jobs and gave the city hope.

The finished bridge opened on May 28, 1937. More than 32,000 cars crossed the bridge that first day. Now, more than 120,000 cars cross it daily. Some people say that the bridge was actually made of gold because it shimmers in the sunlight. This, of course, is only because of paint.

HOTS Analyze

What do you think made Strauss so sure he could build the bridge?

Apply It

Read the passage. Look for problems and solutions as you read. Answer the questions on the next page.

To the Rescue!

While many dogs spend their days playing and having fun, others have very important jobs to do. Some dogs assist people who cannot see or hear. Others help people who cannot walk or move around easily. Today, some of the most skilled dogs are trained for one special purpose—to rescue people from fallen buildings.

Buildings can fall down for a number of reasons. Earthquakes, tornadoes, and hurricanes can do incredible damage to buildings, causing them to collapse. After an accident, rescue efforts must start quickly so that rescue dogs can get right to work.

The site of a fallen building is a dangerous place. There are sharp objects and parts of the building everywhere. How do rescue dogs search through this without hurting themselves? They are trained to walk on uneven surfaces. They learn how to balance on wobbly areas and take small, safe steps.

Another serious problem at the site of a fallen building is the possibility of having people lost or trapped under the rubble. Dog trainers are aware of this issue. Therefore, during their training, rescue dogs are taught how to sense that a human is nearby, using sound and smell. They are lowered down into holes and are taught how to climb ladders, as well.

Often, there is a lot of repair work going on at the site of a fallen building. This can be very noisy and chaotic. Because of this, trainers teach their dogs to ignore loud noises.

In the end, when it comes to saving lives, rescue dogs can be heroes.

Answer these questions about "To the Rescue!" Write your answers in complete sentences.

1. Which details in the first paragraph tell you some important jobs that dogs do?

   _____

   _____

2. What are some problems that occur at the site of a fallen building?

   _____

   _____

3. Why do trainers have to think about problems when they train rescue dogs?

   _____

   _____

4. How are rescue dogs trained to respond to the loud noises of repair work at the site of a fallen building?

   _____

   _____

5. How does finding problems and solutions in the passage help readers understand more about the work rescue dogs do?

   _____

   _____

Compare and Contrast Primary and Secondary Sources

Learn About It

When we read, we get information from many different types of sources. A **primary source** is written about an idea or event at the time the event took place. Diaries, speeches, letters, news footage, and interviews are all examples of primary sources. A **secondary source** is an account of an event which interprets the information provided by primary sources. Textbooks, articles, biographies, encyclopedias, and history books are all secondary sources.

Read the three passages below. Compare the information in the passages.

Passage 1

On July 20, 1969, astronaut Neil Armstrong walked on the moon. It was a big step for both the United States and for the world. It put an end to the "space race" that had begun years before and began a time of exploration.

Passage 2

"I believe that this nation should commit itself to achieving this goal, before this decade is out, of landing a man on the moon and returning him safely to the Earth."
—President John F. Kennedy, 1961

Passage 3

"That's one small step for man, one giant leap for mankind."
—Neil Armstrong, 1969

Passage	Type of Source	Evidence
Passage 1	Secondary	Secondhand account of an event
Passage 2	Primary	Actual quote
Passage 3	Primary	Actual quote

Try It

Read the passages. Think about the information in both sources and how it is presented. Use the questions to help you.

The Fight for Independence

A colony is a region ruled by another country. America was once made up of thirteen colonies. They were ruled by Great Britain. In 1776, the colonies decided that they wanted to be their own country. They declared war against Great Britain. It was a dangerous risk to take. The war would be a long and bloody one. What were some of the events that led to this decision? Did all the colonists agree with it?

Is this passage a primary or secondary source? How do you know?

The king and Parliament, who were the lawmakers of Great Britain, had the power to make laws for the colonies. They had the power to decide what taxes the people in the colonies had to pay. One of the taxes was the Stamp Act, a tax on books, newspapers, and any other printed material. Another was the Sugar Act, which was a tax on sugar.

Colonists no longer wanted to follow British laws or pay British taxes. They felt that the laws they followed should be made by people they themselves had elected. They wanted to make their own taxes. Many colonists did not believe that Great Britain should have the right to tax people who did not elect them. They were arguing against "taxation without representation."

There were some colonists who did not agree. Approximately one in three colonists was still loyal to Great Britain. These "loyalists" were grateful for all that Great Britain had provided. These people felt that the protection of Great Britain was important. They considered themselves British and did not want to fight in a war against Great Britain.

Both Sides

James Otis, a Boston lawyer, wrote this essay in support of the colonists:

I have waited for years to hear some friend of the colonies pleading for [Great Britain]. I have waited in vain. One privilege after another is taken away. Where we shall end up only God knows . . .

To say that the Parliament has . . . power does not make sense. Parliament cannot make two and two equal five. Parliament can declare that something is being done for the good of the whole, but this declaration . . . does not make it true.

> The colonists had reasons for their decision to revolt against Great Britain. What were these reasons? How does the essay by James Otis reflect these reasons?

Martin Howard, a Rhode Island lawyer, spoke for those loyal to Great Britain:

The political rights of the colonies . . . depend completely on the charters which first established them.

I am aware that this reasoning will be argued against by quoting the saying, "No English subject can be taxed without his consent, or the consent of his representatives."

> The loyalists also had reasons against the decision. Does this primary source reflect them? How?

It is the opinion of the [government of Great Britain] that they are the representatives of all British subjects, wherever they may live.

Believe me, my friend, it causes me great pain to see that the colonies are so ungrateful to the mother country, whose army and money have just rescued them . . .

How do the primary sources persuade readers?

Apply It

Read the passages. Think about how the events are described. Answer the questions that follow.

The Oregon Trail

In the 1800s, thousands of people caught what was called "Oregon Fever." This was the overwhelming desire to pack up and move out west. These people traveled along the Oregon Trail, which was a route that joined several towns along the Missouri River to valleys in Oregon. Long lines of covered wagons pulled by oxen traveled 2,000 miles over the harsh terrain. They moved like slow ships across the plain in lines that could be several miles in length.

The travelers were looking forward to starting a new life. Some wanted land of their own. Others thought that the move would bring them new freedoms. Still others were just looking for adventure. Whatever the reason they were going, they all faced the same hardships on the journey.

By making this cross-country trip, many people were leaving homes and friends they were not likely to ever see again. The trip was long, tiring, and dangerous. Their days were spent choking on dust as they walked behind their wagons. The wagon caravans traveled about fifteen to twenty miles a day in the heat, rain, and snow. Many were unable to face these hardships and turned back. Others became sick and died.

Women were expected to cook meals, wash and mend clothes, and care for young children during the journey. Men drove the wagons, cared for animals, hunted for food, and planned routes. Children were also called upon to do their share of the work. They helped their parents care for their younger brothers and sisters and lent a helping hand whenever one was needed.

Pioneer Diaries

"Today we started across the dreary plains. Sad are the thoughts that steal over [my] mind. I am leaving my home, my early friends, never to see them again . . . Hard indeed that heart that does not drop a tear as these thoughts roll across the mind."

—Elizabeth Goltra, Oregon, 1853

"The women helped pitch the tents, helped unload, and helped with yoking up the cattle. Some of the women did nearly all the yoking, many times the men were off away from camp . . . One time, my father was away hunting cattle . . . and that left Mother and the children to attend to everything."

—Martha Ann Morrison, 13 years old

"That this journey is tiresome no one will doubt, that it is perilous, the deaths of many will testify. The heart has a thousand misgivings, and the mind is tortured with anxiety . . ."

—Lodissa Frizzel, 1852

Answer these questions about "The Oregon Trail" and "Pioneer Diaries." Write your answers in complete sentences.

1. What is the topic described in both passages?

   _____

   _____

2. What is one detail in the secondary source that describes the hardships people suffered?

   _____

   _____

3. What is one detail in the primary sources that describes the hardships people suffered?

   _____

   _____

4. How are the kinds of information given in the primary sources and secondary source different?

   _____

   _____

5. How do the primary sources help readers understand the event?

   _____

   _____

Drawings

Learn About It

When we read different texts, we get information in many different ways. Information can be presented to us in **drawings**, such as charts, graphs, diagrams, and timelines. This information helps us better understand what we read by presenting it in a different format.

Look at the timeline. Think about the information it contains.

Average Life Spans

30 days	3 years	12–15 years	65 Years
Mosquito	Rat	Dog	Elephant

Graph	Shows how two or more things are related, how things change over time, or how things compare to one another
Chart	Classifies information under headings or categories
Timeline	Arranges information in chronological order or the order of events
Diagram	Shows how something is put together or how parts relate to one another

Try It

Read the passage. Think about the information in the text and the diagram as you read. Use the questions to help you.

Take a Taste

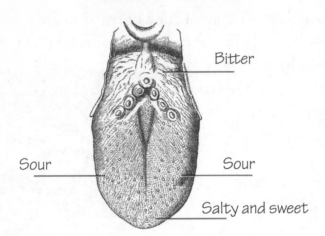

Bitter

Sour   Sour

Salty and sweet

How do we know what is happening around us at any given point? We have help from our five senses— sight, hearing, touch, smell, and taste. One of the most interesting of these senses is our sense of taste.

> The diagram shows where the taste buds are located on the tongue. How does this information help you understand what you read?

Your tongue is the sense organ for taste. It is covered with thousands of tiny taste buds. When you eat something, the saliva in your mouth helps break down the food. This causes the taste buds to send messages through your body to your brain. These messages help your brain know what foods taste like and also aid in the process of digestion.

Why do some foods taste different than others? This is because there are four different kinds of taste buds, located on different parts of your tongue. They are able to taste four basic flavors: sweet, sour, bitter, and salty. The diagram above shows you where the taste buds for each type of flavor are located.

The temperature and texture of foods affects the way they taste, as well. Hot and cold foods taste differently, just like crunchy and smooth foods do.

> The text tells you that taste buds can detect four different, basic flavors. Find this in the passage and name the four basic flavors.

Why does it make sense that hot food might taste different than cold food?

Apply It

Read the passage. Look at the picture and the chart. Answer the questions on the next page.

How Hard or Soft?

All rocks are made up of a combination of two or more minerals. However, not all rocks are the same. Different rocks have different properties. A property is something you can observe. One property of a rock is its hardness, or how hard or soft it is. You can test for the hardness of a rock by following the instructions below.

1. Gather these materials:
    *   glass plate
    *   penny
    *   nail
    *   permanent marker
    *   4 rocks
    *   masking tape

2. Make a chart like this one:

Rock	Fingernail	Penny	Nail	Glass
A				
B				
C				
D				

3. Use the masking tape and marker to label each rock: A, B, C, and D.
4. Try to scratch each rock with your fingernail, the penny, and the nail. Record your results on the chart.
5. Try to scratch the glass with each rock. Record your results on the chart.

Which rocks were you able to scratch with your fingernail? Which rocks scratched the glass? Which rock is the hardest?

Answer these questions about "How Hard or Soft?" Write your answers in complete sentences.

1. What does the picture show? How is it related to the passage?

_____

_____

2. Charts help you analyze information. How will this chart help you when you have finished the experiment?

_____

_____

3. What other objects might you use to test the hardness of the rocks?

_____

_____

4. How do drawings such as charts or timelines help readers better understand passages?

_____

_____

_____

_____

Reasons and Evidence

Learn About It

> **Reasons** tell readers *why* they should accept some information or an opinion. An **opinion** is an individual's personal belief about a subject that cannot be proven to be true or false. **Evidence** supplies *proof* for reasons. Reasons and evidence are used to convince someone to believe or act in a certain way.

Read the passage. See if the reasons and evidence convince you.

The sidewalks of our town could use a cleanup. Teenagers are the perfect people for this job! Store owners should hire them to keep the areas in front of the stores clean. Kids can pick up litter and sweep. Experts say that a clean storefront attracts more shoppers. Additionally, the kids can spend the money they earn in the stores!

Element	What It Does	Example
Reason	Tells readers why they should accept some information or an opinion	The kids can spend the money they earn in the stores!
Evidence	Supplies proof for your reasons	Clean areas attract shoppers.
Opinion	Offers an individual's personal belief about a subject	The sidewalks of our town could use a cleanup.

Try It

Read the passage. Underline the reasons and evidence that persuade you. Use the questions to help you.

Bike Safety

Bike riding is enjoyable for people of all ages. It is a fun way to exercise and to get around. Going for bike rides is a great way families can spend time together. However, it is important to remember that a bike is *not* a toy—it is a vehicle. Because of this, there are safety rules you must follow when riding your bike.

> The writer states that a bike is not a toy. What is the reason provided?

First, you must always wear a helmet. No matter how short the ride is, it is always a good idea. In many states, it is the law. This is because many bike accidents involve head injuries and the damage is often serious. Every year, about half a million kids are injured in bike accidents. Most of these injuries could have been avoided if the riders had been wearing a helmet.

Additionally, it is important that you are visible when you are riding a bike. Just because you can see a driver doesn't mean the driver can see you! Wearing dull colors is not a good idea. Instead, wear bright colors or something that reflects light.

> The writer provides evidence that wearing a helmet is a good idea. What is this evidence?

Control is important when steering a bike. Having only one hand on the handlebars is not enough. If you need to carry something while riding your bike, put it in a backpack. Never share your bike seat with a friend or ride on the handlebars of someone else's bike. It is too easy to lose your balance and fall.

Lastly, road hazards can be very dangerous for bicyclists. Watch out for potholes, gravel, puddles, leaves, animals, and broken glass.

What are some other ways a rider might make sure to be seen by drivers?

Apply It

Read the passage. Look for reasons and evidence as you read. Answer the questions on the next page.

More Trees!

To the Editor:

When you picture the streets of our town, what do you see? Do you see a dull landscape of just buildings, sidewalks, stores, and schools? Shouldn't trees be part of this picture? I think so, which is why I believe that we need to start a tree-planting program in our town.

It is true that we have many trees in our town parks. But why should we have to go to parks to get the benefits of trees? Trees are beautiful to look at and are good for our health. They provide shade, cut traffic noise, and cheer people up!

More trees throughout town will benefit our health. Trees give off oxygen and help fight pollution. The leaves of trees provide shade and make the streets cooler. Sitting on a sidewalk bench under the shade of a tree on a summer afternoon is a comfort to many people. Planting trees along busy roads will muffle, or cut down, traffic noises that have been increasing every year. The beauty of the trees during every season will cheer people at all times of year.

The town council will be meeting on June 3. It will be voting on the budget for next year. We do not need to use the entire budget for roads and traffic signs. Shouldn't some of it go toward planting more trees, in order to make our town healthier, quieter, cooler, and prettier? What could be better? Please take this into consideration.

Thank you,
Abby Holmes

Answer these questions about "More Trees!" Write your answers in complete sentences.

1. What does the writer of the letter want the town to do? How does the title of the passage support this?

2. Name one reason the writer gives in the second paragraph for planting trees.

3. What evidence about trees and pollution does the writer give in the third paragraph?

4. What reason does the writer give for planting trees along busy roads?

5. What reason or evidence in the passage will most likely make you agree with the writer?

Graphic Organizers

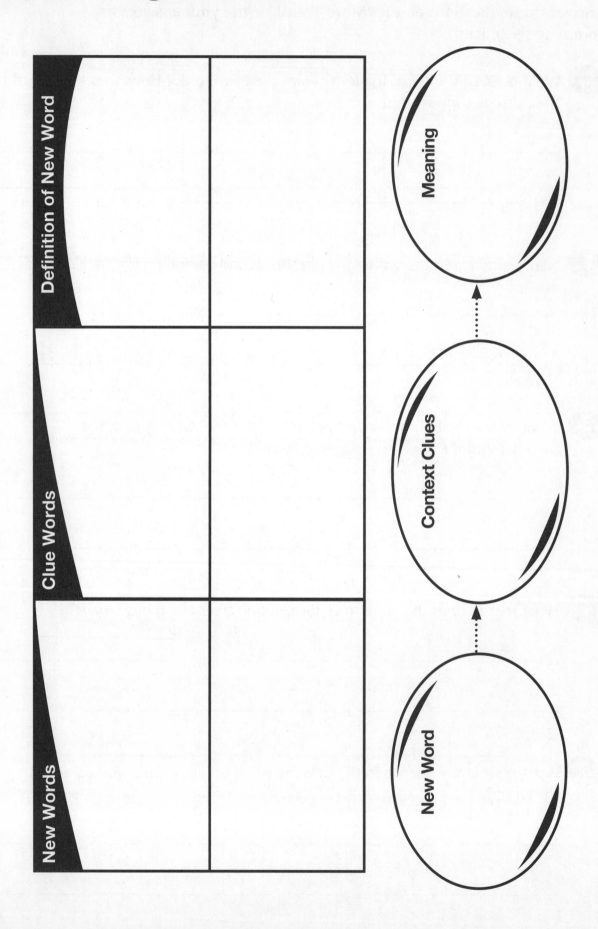

Definition of New Word

Clue Words

New Words

Meaning

Context Clues

New Word

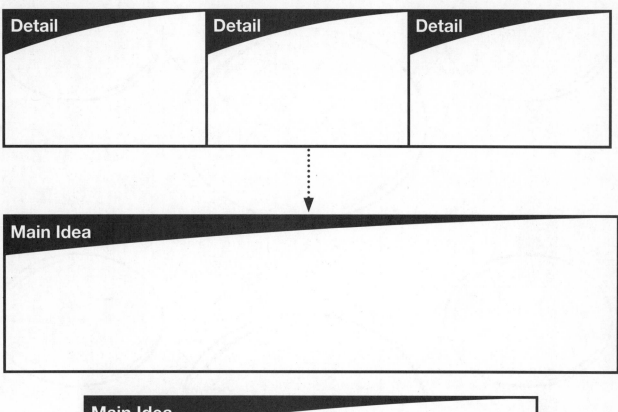

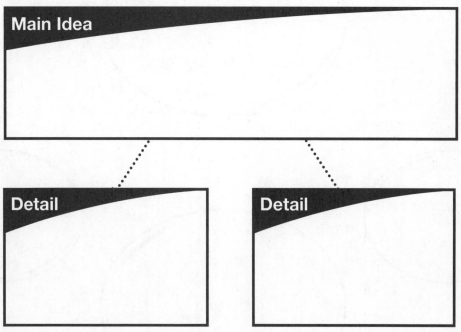

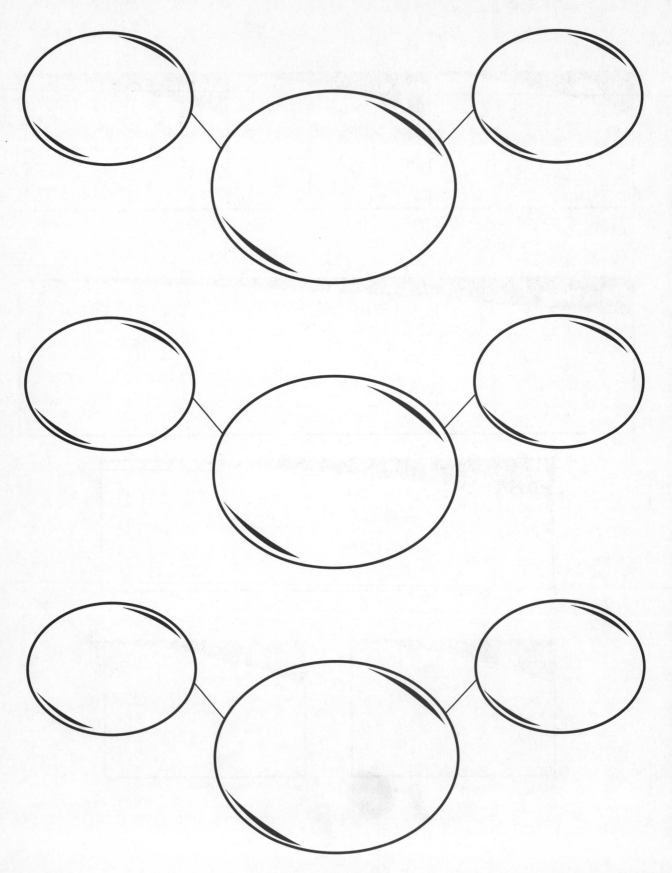